# contents

## Stories

## Features

## Puzzles

## Posters

P74

P62

P126

P24

P5

Printed and published in Great Britain by D. C. THOMSON & CO., LTD., 185 Fleet Street, London EC41 2HS. © D. C. THOMSON & CO., LTD., 2005.
*While every reasonable care will be taken, neither D. C. Thomson & Co., Ltd., nor its agents accept any liability for loss or damage to colour transparencies or any other material submitted to this publication.*
ISBN 1 84535 044 8

# Penny's Place

*P*enny Jordan's parents owned three café's — Penny's Place and Penny's in Chesterford, and a beach café in Spain. After school, Penny and her mates, Donna, Sita, Arlene and Gemma, always met up in Penny's Place. One evening Arlene arrived with her twin brother —

Hi, guys. Mind if Pete joins us today? He's fallen out with his mates.

No probs, Arlene. Good to see you, Pete.

So what was the falling out over?

There's this new guy, Gary. He's just stirring things up.

Yeah. And he thinks he's great, too, Penny.

But, a few days later —

Hi, girls. Meet my mate Gary.

Oh, er — hi, Gary.

What's goin' on here?

And you can go as well, Arlene. You're all three barred.

But, Ma, it wasn't Arlene's fault.

*The next day —*

I'm sorry about what happened yesterday. Gary was really out of order.

Yeah, it wasn't your fault, Pete. I'm sure once Ma's calmed down, you and Arlene will be allowed in again.

I'll speak to *my* mum, too. I'm sure she'll say you can come back.

But —

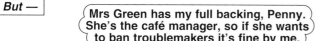

Mrs Green has my full backing, Penny. She's the café manager, so if she wants to ban troublemakers it's fine by me.

*Later —*

That was the police on the phone. 'Penny's Place' is on fire. It looks as if it's been started deliberately.

Oh, no.

This will have something to do with that Arlene and Pete business I'll be bound, Penny.

No way, Mum. Arlene and Pete are my mates. They wouldn't have anything to do with something like this.

Though I can't vouch for Gary.

*The next day —*

What a mess. It'll take ages to put things right.

Yeah. But at least Penny's folks have insurance to cover the costs. My poor mum's out of a job until it's all up and running again.

7

On Monday —

So what's on for later, girls? Is it straight home, or has anyone any suggestions on where we can meet up?

Straight home, I think. Everywhere else is either too posh or too packed.

That's where you're wrong, Sita. Come home my way this afternoon and see what I've found.

So —

It's a bit old-fashioned, but it's cheap, clean and not too crowded. Plus my gran says they do great cakes and crumpets.

Okay, let's give it a try.

BOBBY'S

I see what you mean about it being old-fashioned.

Gran says she doesn't know how they make a living. The place is always half empty.

I'm sorry, but we only allow two school children in at a time.

Oh, but we won't be any bother. I'm Penny Jordan. My parents own 'Penny's' and 'Penny's Place'.

9

*Over the next few days Penny made it a regular thing.*

If you sold a wider range of soft drinks people would have more choice. And you could fill rolls with more salads and offer vegetarian choices. Mum finds they sell really well.

We-ell . . . if you give me a hand I could give it a try.

*Shirley cooked really tasty food —*

Home Made Veggie Burgers and Quiche.

I'm sure Mum would love to sell some of this in her café.

*Trade soon picked up —*

We've put the word out about how good this place is, Penny.

I can see that. We're really busy.

How's Bobby today, Shirley?

He's getting there, Penny. But the truth is we want to sell up and retire to somewhere hot — like Spain — but we can't afford to.

*Then, one afternoon —*

Woops some of Mum's customers are coming in now. Hope she won't mind.

*So Penny suggested her mum sample the food, too.*

Perhaps I will, Penny. It's always good to keep an eye on the opposition.

They're hardly that, Mum. But I'm sure you'll really like Shirley and Bobby.

*The next day —*

Look, Penny, that might be a job for Donna's mum until we can take her on again.

Good idea, Mum.

*And —*

Well? What do you think of Shirley's cooking?

Everything's wonderful. No wonder people are coming here.

Thanks, my dear. But I've been doing it for years. I do love cooking.

Would you supply my coffee shop, too? I'd pay you well of course.

I'd love to — provided I can find lunchtime help, that is.

I think we can help there, too. Mrs Green would love the job.

*And —*

Oh, 'Bobby's' is packed out. Looks like we'll have to wait for a table.

Yeah. Mum says they've been really busy all week. She's been working lots of extra hours.

*Then, just as things were going really well —*

'Penny's Place' refurbishment is finished. We can open again.

But what about 'Bobby's Café', Dad?

THE END

Best Friends

# MUMS

## A mum is someone who...

...turns down the TV whenever your favourite pop programme comes on....

...won't let the dog sleep on your bed, even although he's your best friend and he's cold and lonely...

...always has to have the last word in any argument...

...wants you to eat everything on your plate before you get a biscuit...

...saves her weirdest outfits for wearing to parents' evening at school...

...refuses to do your washing until you tidy your room...

...is always there when you need her – no matter *what* time it is!

**And that's why we love 'em!**

16

18

19

Then —

I've just got to pick up Mum's magazine.

Okay. I'll wait out here.

Me, too.

And, when Kay came back out —

Where's Dan?

Gone.

Gone? Where? Why?

Look, Kay he told me he was only being nice to you so he could get to know *me* better. While you were in the shop he asked me out, so I told him to get lost!

Huh! Like I believe *that!* You're just jealous. All you want to do is mess up my life. Having a stepsister like you is the worst thing that's ever happened to me.

Please yourself, Kay. Go and ask Dan if you want. He can't have gone far.

I will.

And —

Hey, hang on a minute, Dan. I thought you wanted to walk home with me.

Sorry, change of plan.

21

But I thought you liked me? I thought . . .

Gimme a break! Like I'd be interested in a kid like you! It was your stepsister I fancied. Okay?

So Liz was telling the truth. Dan's nothing but a rat! But I was horrid to her so she'll probably never want to speak to me again.

But —

Oh, Liz I-I'm really pleased to see you. And I'm sorry I was so rude when you were just looking out for me.

Forget it! Let's put that creep Dan down to experience and start again, shall we?

You see, I've always wanted a little sister . . .

You have?

Yeah! Cos it doesn't mean just sharing a room, it means sharing problems, too — and sharing chores!

Good point, Liz. Maybe this sisterly thing isn't quite so bad, after all.

THE END

# THE NAME GAME!

This'll keep you busy! Can you find the 70 names listed here in our mega wordsearch? They can read up, down, backwards, forwards or diagonally, and letters can be used more than once.

## HAPPY HUNTING!

| | | | |
|---|---|---|---|
| Amy | Angela | Anne | Beatrice |
| Bella | Bethany | Candy | Caroline |
| Cheryl | Dawn | Diana | Donna |
| Eleanor | Emily | Emma | Fiona |
| Flora | Frances | Gail | Gina |
| Grace | Hannah | Harriet | Helen |
| Ingrid | Ida | Isla | Jane |
| Jenny | Jessica | Kate | Keira |
| Kelly | Laura | Louise | Lucy |
| Marian | Melanie | Milly | Naomi |
| Natalie | Nicole | Olga | Olivia |
| Orla | Patsy | Paula | Phoebe |
| Rachel | Rebecca | Ruth | Sal |
| Serena | Suzie | Tamsin | Theresa` |
| Tina | Una | Ursula | Victoria |
| Violet | Virginia | Wanda | Wendy |
| Winifred | Yolanda | Yvonne | Zara |
| Zipporah | Zoe | | |

| | | | | | | | | | | | | | | | | | | | | |
|---|---|---|---|---|---|---|---|---|---|---|---|---|---|---|---|---|---|---|---|---|
| Y | C | U | L | F | L | E | V | S | A | N | K | G | A | E | G | Z | A | L |
| P | Y | L | L | I | M | C | S | I | W | D | A | E | N | Y | I | K | S | O |
| V | I | C | T | O | R | I | A | A | R | I | N | I | I | I | P | N | E | E | U |
| A | L | R | O | N | M | R | D | Q | L | G | L | A | P | R | A | L | C | I |
| A | R | Y | N | A | H | T | E | B | T | O | I | O | L | K | A | L | N | S |
| Y | N | O | R | O | N | A | M | Y | R | A | R | N | A | O | Y | Y | A | E |
| P | D | I | N | F | E | E | H | A | L | A | M | T | I | R | Y | W | R | A |
| I | A | N | T | A | L | B | C | M | H | A | E | S | E | A | O | I | F | L |
| N | N | S | E | R | E | N | A | O | E | I | I | H | I | L | W | N | S | E |
| O | L | G | A | W | H | L | M | Q | R | L | C | V | A | N | F | I | U | G |
| A | S | E | R | E | H | T | E | R | U | E | A | U | I | L | P | F | Z | N |
| J | E | S | S | I | C | A | A | N | R | Y | R | N | O | L | L | R | I | A |
| D | O | N | N | A | D | H | L | A | S | A | S | R | I | R | O | E | E | Y |
| H | A | N | N | A | H | E | N | T | U | A | A | V | E | E | U | D | B | D |
| E | E | R | U | T | H | A | A | A | L | S | I | B | J | A | N | E | E | N |
| N | M | C | N | C | I | P | R | L | A | O | E | N | N | O | V | Y | O | A |
| N | N | I | A | D | N | A | W | I | L | C | E | L | O | C | I | N | H | C |
| A | S | R | L | R | Z | T | D | E | C | O | A | N | A | L | U | A | P | T |
| J | E | N | N | Y | Y | G | A | T | A | Z | N | A | O | M | I | E | M | M | A |

23

# All About...ORLANDO

He once broke his back when he fell from a third floor balcony. Doctors thought he might not walk again but, thankfully, he made a full recovery.

His favourite foods include pasta, pizza, potatoes, spinach and rice.

Orlando loves trying out weird and wonderful sports like bungee jumping, skydiving, snowboarding and paragliding.

At school, Orlando passed 8 O levels and 3 A Levels. He graduated from the Guildhall School of Music and Drama with a BA(Hons) in 1999.

Orlando was 16 when he moved from Caterbury, Kent, to London. Once there, he joined the National Youth Theatre.

The otherwise almost perfect Mr Bloom has been known to bite his nails. Blee!

Orlando was born on January 13, 1977, making him a cool Capricorn.

He has a sister, Samantha, who is two years older than he is.

Orlando stands at 1.80m tall.

His favourite colour is yellow.

His full name is Orlando Jonathan Blanchard Bloom.

While filming 'Lord of The Rings', Orlando fell from his horse and broke a rib.

The young Orlando appeared in episodes of 'Casualty' and 'Midsomer Murders'.

Apart from his back and his rib, Mr Accident-Prone has also broken his nose, two legs, an arm, a wrist, a finger, and a toe. He has also cracked his skull three times.

When they were young, Orlando and his sister used to win reciting competitions.

One of his favourite actors is Johnny Depp.

Orlando isn't fond of computers – in fact, he doesn't like them at all.

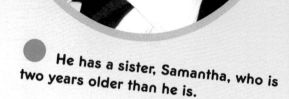

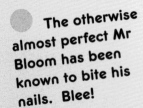
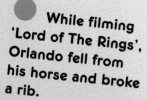

# Angel

WHEN Angela Hamilton, a young girl from a wealthy Victorian family, discovered that she had a fatal illness, she decided to dedicate the remainder of her life to rescuing homeless waifs. In the years following her death, many of the orphans returned to lay flowers at her memorial statue and, one morning —

Good morning, my dear. I haven't seen you at Miss Angel's memorial before.

Peter and I were both rescued by Miss Angel, but you are too young to have known her.

You are right. But although I may not be able to remember Miss Angel, I have good reason to be grateful to her, too.

My story begins at Christmas, after Miss Angel had set up the stablehouse home for her waifs.

It's late, Miss Angel. Surely you ain't going out now! It's Christmas Eve!

Exactly, Alfie! And I can make sure that a few of the poor and starving go to sleep tonight with food in their stomachs.

You're a good 'un, Miss Angel. I'll come, too, and carry the basket of food.

I would be grateful, Alfie. My arms are so tired . . .

Works 'erself too hard, Miss Angel does. But she won't stop.

"They visited many homeless children that night. And, much later, in a cold, damp railway arch —"

Ta! Merry Christmas to you, Miss Angel!

And to you, too, Bessie.

I will be back tomorrow. I hope you manage to sleep tonight.

Not likely. There's been a baby born round here, and it kept me awake all last night.

A baby? Where, Bessie?

In the next arch.

Poor mite! This is no place for a new-born baby! I will go and see if the parents need anything.

I cannot hear crying now, Alfie. Perhaps the parents have found themselves a better place to live.

"But then —"

Who's there?

A friend — I bring food. I am told there is a baby here. Are you the father?

Aye, that's right. Sam Kirk's my name. We're new round here.

Where is the baby? I don't hear it crying.

My little girl is too weak to cry now, and my wife is poorly as well. They're dying, miss! Can you help them?

Let me see.

I'm sorry. Only a trained doctor or nurse can help here. But I will go for assistance.

Don't bother. We can't afford medical fees. If *you* can't help them, there's no hope.

Forget about the fees. Keep your wife and baby warm. I will be back shortly.

*"Miss Angel ran for the nearest doctor —"*

They're here, in this archway.

*"But, after a brief examination —"*

They can be saved — but they need to be treated in hospital. It will cost a lot of money.

Fetch a carriage, Doctor. Take them there. I will pay.

*"Miss Angel went back to the stablehouse —"*

I have already sold most of my jewels to buy food and clothing for my waifs. But there is still one thing . . .

. . . this emerald necklace which my dear mama and papa gave me last Christmas.

THE END

# Simply Style!

## YOU WILL NEED...

Plain hair clips
Nail varnish to match your outfit
Glitter

If you're stuck for hair clips to match a favourite outfit, then never fear cos we'll show you how you can turn the plainest accessories into top style. And it only takes minutes!

**1.** Paint the hair clips with your chosen nail varnish.

**2.** While the varnish is still wet, sprinkle with glitter, being careful not to put on too much.

**3.** Leave the clips to dry thoroughly, then give them a gentle shake to remove any loose glitter. If you want to brighten up plain metal clips without changing the colour, then paint them with clear varnish and sprinkle on glitter as before.

And there you have it.
Instant accessories to match any outfit.

"Still dreaming about Paul?" Stacy, her best friend, popped up beside her. "Why can't you just ask him out and get it over with?"

"I can't do that," Taz replied, cheeks reddening. "What if he says no?"

"He won't," Stacy replied, confidently. "Jamie says he's crazy about you."

"Jamie **would** say that — he just wants to make me look stupid." Taz threw her hands in the air. "Anyway, if Paul's crazy about me, why doesn't he ask me out?"

"He's probably shy," Stacy argued. "Everyone knows he likes you. I bet he's even told his mum!"

"Don't be stupid!" Taz snapped. "Anyway, let's not waste all day talking about Paul Hill. There are lots of better things to do — like going in there!" Taz pointed towards a fortune-teller's tent tucked away in a corner of the field. "D'you fancy giving it a go, Stace? It's only £2."

Stacy frowned.

"No way! I'm not paying £2 to hear a load of made-up rubbish. I'd rather go for a hot dog," she said. "I'll meet you over at the tea tent in twenty minutes."

Inside the dimly lit tent, Taz settled herself on a small stool in front of a heavily draped table. A red lamp hung above her head, casting just enough light for her to make out a heavily veiled woman sitting behind a crystal ball.

T AZ strolled amongst the marquees, rides and game stalls, listening to the music and licking an ice cream. She usually loved the school's end of term summer fair, seeing it as a great chance to hang around with all her mates. But this year it was different. This year the only person she wanted to see was Paul Hill — but he always disappeared when she was around, like he was scared or something. Taz still hadn't got to talk to him, and she wouldn't get another chance until school started again in September — unless she got lucky today! Her eyes searched the teeming crowd, hopefully.

# TUNE-TELLER

Spooky! Taz thought nervously as she stared at the fortune-teller. She was pretty sure it was one of the teachers in disguise, but it was impossible to recognise her.

Before Taz could move, a strong hand had clamped hers in an iron grasp. This woman was weird — really over the top.

"I see a romantic soul," the fortune-teller cooed softly. "I see a longing for love." The figure swayed slightly in the darkness. "I see a boy — a handsome boy. Such a beautiful smile!"

Taz's heart started to beat a little faster. She opened her mouth but, before she could speak, the woman interrupted.

"He loves you, my dear," the woman patted her hand. "But he is afraid to speak."

Taz's head was spinning. Paul actually loved her! Then she went cold! **Someone** loved her! But she couldn't be sure it was Paul! She shuddered — what if it were that prat Simms from maths class?

"You've got to tell me more," she encouraged the woman, breathlessly.

Dark, almond-shaped eyes glittered above the heavy green veil, then lowered to gaze into the crystal ball.

"I see a letter P." The eyes flicked

back to Taz. "Am I right?"

"Oh, yes!" Taz replied, excitedly. "Is he going to ask me out?"

The masked figure shook her head, sadly. "He thinks you don't like him."

"But I do!" Taz exclaimed.

"Then you must tell him." The woman patted her hand once more. "You must find him — now! The stars are perfect for you to get together!"

Taz jumped to her feet, fumbling in her pocket for a two-pound coin. She threw it on to the table, muttering her thanks.

"Go quickly before it's too late!" the woman hissed.

Blinded and blinking, Taz stumbled out into the bright sunshine. The first thing she saw as her eyes got used to the light was Paul Hill walking straight towards her.

"Paul," she gasped! "This has to be starred — just like the fortune-teller said!"

Before she knew what she was doing, she had stepped towards him and placed a hand on his arm.

"Hi, Paul!" She took a big breath. "I — er — I wondered if you'd like to go for a milkshake or something?"

Paul's eyebrows rose with surprise, then his smile widened.

"I'd love to."

"Great!" Taz let out a deep breath! She couldn't believe she'd just done that! She'd actually asked Paul Hill out — and he had just said yes!

"But I'll have to give my mum her lunch first," Paul said, waving a sandwich box. "It won't take a minute."

"I've never met your mum," Taz replied, scanning the crowd. "Where is she?"

"In that tent," Paul replied, pointing a finger. "She's the fortune-teller."

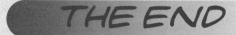
THE END

33

Best
Friends

# A Dream Come True

**F**or as long as she could remember, Hannah Armitage's dream had been to be a ballerina.

Just go over those steps again before you go home, girls.

I'd give anything to go to a proper ballet school, but I know Mum and Dad couldn't possibly afford it.

Hannah! I'd like to have a word with you.

Oh, no! The lesson can't be nearly over already? Time just seems to fly by when I'm dancing.

How would you like to try for a scholarship at the Rosetta Dance Academy? You've a lot of talent.

I'd love to. It's one of the top ballet schools. I'm sure Mum and Dad will let me give it a go.

Two weeks later —

Fantastic! I've been accepted for an audition. I've to go there for a weekend and see how I get on.

Hannah Armitage! You'll be sharing a room with two other girls in the west wing. I'll show you the way.

Thank you.

This is a brilliant place. It'll be a dream come true if I'm accepted as a pupil!

Huh! What a drag. I'd rather watch TV. But I suppose I'd better go along with you.

To think that all these great ballerinas were here as pupils! It's a privilege to be allowed to audition here.

Nicola's just trying to make a good impression in front of Madame Yvette.

Later —

Mum thought I might starve this weekend, so she packed up all these goodies for me! Dig in — I daren't take anything home again!

Thanks, Hannah!

Food! Cool!

Nicola's not too snooty to try out Mum's baking! Maybe sharing will make her more friendly.

But, at bedtime —

Breakfast is at eight tomorrow. Madame Yvette said she wanted everyone to be on time, as she's taking a class for us at nine.

Right! I'll set my alarm for half-past seven.

Oh, Nicola's case is crammed full of chocolate and crisps. So much for sharing.

I'm too excited to sleep. I *must* do well tomorrow! I'll never have another chance like this.

38

Finally, it was Hannah's turn —

I'll do my best. I've nothing to lose now.

It's a pity there aren't two scholarships so Stephanie and I could both come here. I think she'd be a great friend.

After the auditions —

It was an extremely hard decision as you all show great promise. However we look for something special in the girls we choose, so our choice is Hannah Armitage.

Me! Oh, that's wonderful! But — but why . . .?

Because you're kind, friendly and helpful — as well as a good dancer. You see, I'm *already* a pupil here and I was put in with you to see who'd best fit in with the school. We don't want cheats and bigheads here.

Oh, Stephanie. It's my dream come true!

So, at the beginning of the next term —

Hannah! It's great to see you again!

I'm the luckiest girl alive — to have a place at the Rosetta Academy *and* a friend like Stephanie!

THE END

41

# go with

## What's Your Hot Holiday?
## Follow our flowchart to find out!

**START**

Are you scared of creepy-crawlies?

You prefer the countryside to the city. True?

Do you like sleeping in a sleeping bag?

Are you good at memorising facts and figures?

You hate history at school! True?

Do you catch cold easily?

You wouldn't mind going without a shower for a few days. True?

Do you enjoy picnics?

Do you get bored lying in the sun?

Do you love the smell of the sea?

Could you be described as lazy?

Do you get travelsick?

You'd love to swim with dolphins! True?

Do you hate the feeing of wet sand between your toes?

# the flow!

**Do you long to visit places you read about in magazines and books?**

**Do you burn easily in the sun?**

**Would sleeping outside in a tent seem like a big adventure?**

**You love the smoky smell of burning wood. True?**

**Are you scared of bats?**

**You'd love to see a fox or badger in the wild. True?**

**Do you enjoy walking?**

**Do you hate the sticky feel of sun cream?**

**Do you hate when waves wet your face and head?**

Y N

## SIGHT-SEEING SISTER –

You just adore seeing the sights and don't mind travelling miles to see smoking volcanoes, gushing waterfalls, old castles or quaint local villages. You find something interesting in just about anything you see.

## CAMPING QUEEN –

Animals, flowers, trees, rivers – you love anything to do with nature. Camping in the wild is your idea of heaven and you'd love to sit by a campfire beneath the stars, watching the bats flying overhead.

## BEACH BABE –

You're a seaside sizzler and your favourite holiday would be spent lying on a sunny, sandy beach, or beside a cool, blue pool. You love swimming and couldn't be happier in the water if you were a mermaid.

# DADS
## A dad is someone who...

...insists on silence whenever the news comes on...

...embarrasses you by wearing his oldest, tattiest shorts to mow the front lawn...

...sulks when his football team loses...

...sits around doing nothing but reading the paper, while you and Mum do all the work...

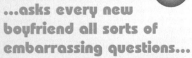

...refuses to eat anything you cook – even before he tastes it...

...asks every new boyfriend all sorts of embarrassing questions...

QUESTIONNAIRE

...buys you special treats when you've run out of pocket money!

### And that's why we love 'em!

# MEET ME!

## HI, I'M LEIGHAN, AND I LIVE IN MORPETH, NORTHUMBERLAND.

When I joined a local Saturday morning stage school a few years ago, I had no idea where it would lead me. But since then I have appeared in a number of stage performances including 'Joseph and his Amazing Technicolour Dreamcoat' at the Empire Theatre in Sunderland.

I have also been lucky enough to appear in a TV drama called 'Distant Shores', when I went on location to some beautiful seaside spots. While filming, I had a caravan of my own to relax in between scenes, a make up artist to put on my make up and a wardrobe assistant

**This is a picture of me with the actor Peter Davidson, who was the star of 'Distant Shores'.**

who looked after my clothes. It was wonderful – even although I didn't get to wear as much make up as I would have liked.

There weren't a lot of lines to learn, but I had to show lots of different emotions. I was treated just like the adults and was expected to be professional and get on with the job like everyone else – no messing about. Everyone helped me a lot and my mum came with me, so I felt quite safe.

TV dramas are well paid and my mum allowed me to spend some of the money on redecorating my room. That's where I keep most of my favourite things – so read on!

I love having my friends round to listen to music, so I keep a good CD collection.

This is the clown my dad bought for me when I was born. He brought it into the hospital for me, so it is very special and I would never part with it.

This is the outfit I wore for my part in the school production of 'Anything Goes'. I played a flapper and danced the Charleston.

Just a minute, this might be my agent calling. Only joking, but I wouldn't be without my mobile phone for *anything*.

I need make up for stage, and I like to experiment in real life, too.

I got this outfit to take on the school trip to Prague, and I love it.

This MP3 player was a very special Christmas present.

McFly! They're my faves!

One thing I don't like is clutter. I hand on all my clothes when I've outgrown them, so my wardrobe is always tidy.

So that's it! I hope you've enjoyed this little peek into my life. And who knows, maybe you'll see me on some other TV programmes in the future.

# Spot the

## Just how like your star sign are you?

**1. Do you love parties?**
a) Yes – you're the life and soul of every gathering!
b) Yes – you love dressing up and meeting people!
c) They're okay – but you'd much rather spend a quiet night in.
d) Yes – but you've got to be in the mood.

**2. Do you daydream a lot?**
b) Not much – there's too much other stuff to think about.
c) Yes – you're always in trouble for not paying attention.
a) Yes – usually about romance or stars you like.
d) No – you're usually too busy.

**3. Would you like to be on TV?**
c) It might be fun – but you'd rather *watch* TV than be on it.
b) As long as it was serious, like the news or a documentary.
a) Yes – you've got star quality.
d) Only if you got well paid for it.

**4. Are you full of ideas?**
a) Yes – life's never quiet while you're around!
b) Yes – you're good at solving problems and thinking up new ways to do things.
d) Yes – mainly on how to make money.
c) Yes – you're very artistic.

**5. What's your fave type of book?**
c) Supernatural or fantasy.
a) Something romantic, or real-life with lots of action.
b) History or geography – anything that makes you think.
d) Something on cookery or craft.

**6. Do you enjoy sport?**
d) Only when you win.
a) Yes – you're a great runner, jumper, catcher, batter….
c) You'd love to be a sports star - but you just don't have the energy.
b) Yes – you do most sports well.

# Signs!

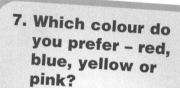

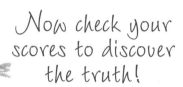

ry our fun quiz to find out.

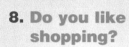

**7. Which colour do you prefer – red, blue, yellow or pink?**

**b)** Not really fussy – but tend to like soft greens and yellows.

**a)** Definitely red – it's so full of life!

**d)** Pastel pinks are your sort of thing.

**c)** Any shade of blue – it's the colour of the sky and the sea.

**8. Do you like shopping?**

**d)** You particularly like to buy things for your room.

**b)** Yes – especially if your best mate goes with you!

**c)** Only if you're looking for something special.

**a)** Clothes, shoes, food - anything at all! You *love* shopping!

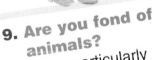

**9. Are you fond of animals?**

**a)** Yes – particularly horses – they're so elegant!

**c)** Yes – you're mad about them!

**d)** They're okay – but you can live without them.

**b)** Yes – animals have feelings like everyone else and should be cared for.

*Now check your scores to discover the truth!*

**Mostly a**
You're very like one of the fire signs – Aries, Sagittarius or Leo. You're noisy, outspoken, honest and adventurous. In fact, you burn so brightly, you put everyone else in the shade!

**Mostly b**
You should be an air sign – Gemini, Aquarius or Libra. You are friendly, gossipy, flirty and very clever. You're so full of life, you make everyone's head spin!

**Mostly c**
You're most like a water sign – Pisces, Scorpio or Cancer. You're dreamy, kind, sensitive, artistic and totally in tune with nature. Your gentle charm enchants the universe!

**Mostly d**
You're typical of an Earth sign – Taurus, Virgo or Capricorn. You are practical, realistic, reliable and patient. Your clear thinking and common sense are the envy of everyone!

Where will it all end, I ask myself? Where will it all end?

Oh, no! Cook's gone all dramatic now. Don't tell me she wants to be in the play, too.

She didn't. But —

Just see this list, Nellie. We've twenty-four for dinner tomorrow. All because of this silly play.

If that includes Mr Salinger, then you'd better make it twenty-seven! He eats like a horse!

In the drawing room —

So it's your opinion that the uprising in the colonies will soon be put down then, sir?

That it will, Sir William, that it will. You can take that as gospel.

Oh, Mr Salinger, how very knowledgeable you are.

Your understanding of world affairs is obvious in Act 2 of 'Christmas At The Palace'. Oh, yes indeed.

Thank you, ladies. I must admit I have yet to see my plays bettered either side of the Atlantic.

I feel I know the character of Princess Carlotta so well. It's as if I share her every thought.

Oh, sister! Those were my very words to you upon rising this morning!

Girls! Girls! I feel sure your dear mama has need of you in the conservatory!

But, Papa . . .

Mr Salinger hasn't even heard us read yet!

51

52

53

54

# Looking Good

*If you have no money for expensive creams and potions, then don't despair! Mum's kitchen cupboards should have everything you need to keep skin, eyes, feet and hair looking gorgeous!*

## SKIN

Before cleansing, break your favourite herbal teabag into a bowl, then add very hot (not boiling) water. Place your face over the bowl, a towel over your head, and relax for ten minutes. Your skin will be warm, glowing and especially easy to cleanse.

If you cleanse your face before you go to bed, you don't need to do it again in the morning. Just rinse with lukewarm water.

To deep cleanse without soap, mix one teaspoon of milk with one teaspoon of honey and massage it into your face. Remember to rinse really well afterwards! If you want a *very* deep cleanse, try adding one tablespoon of oatmeal to the mixture, but be careful to avoid the delicate eye area.

To remove make-up, use a teaspoon of powdered skimmed milk mixed with warm water.

Almond oil is another great make-up remover - plus it moisturises skin, softens hands and soothes sunburn. If you don't have almond oil - or if you're allergic to nuts - try olive oil instead.

A handful of bicarbonate of soda added to the bath water, makes skin silky-smooth and soft.

If you suffer from spots, don't squeeze them as that will only make them worse. Instead, dab them with cool chamomile tea or, if they're sore and red, dab them with witch-hazel to stop infection.

## FEET

Rest tired feet by lying on the floor with your feet higher than your head. Try to do this for at least ten minutes.

If you have rough skin on your feet, try mixing rough sea-salt with a little olive oil and five or six mashed strawberries. Rub the mixture over the feet, then gently wash off to leave your feet feeling much smoother. Alternatively, as the olive oil and salt work almost as well on their own, we suggest you just use them and **eat** the strawberries!

## EYES

Banish puffy eyes by placing cooled, used teabags on them for around ten minutes. Don't forget to wash your face after, though. Likewise, you can soothe tired or sore eyes by covering them with thin slices of raw potato or cucumber.

Herbal infusions can be soothing and two of the best are sage and parsley. To make the infusion, pour boiling water over the fresh or dried leaves. Leave the mixture until it is cold, then strain. Soak cotton wool balls in the liquid and place over the eyes as before.

✳ **Always ask permission before using kitchen equipment.**

# HAIR

Take 125ml of milk and use a clean face cloth to dab it on your hair. Leave for 15 minutes, then rinse out. This should make your hair very soft and shiny.

Add shine to fair or blonde hair by adding two tablespoons of lemon juice to the shampoo. This is also a great treatment for greasy hair.

For frizzy hair, add a tablespoonful of honey to one litre of warm water and then use the mixture to rinse your hair.

A simple conditioning treatment is to comb a little mayonnaise through your hair. Wrap a towel round your head and leave it for 30 minutes before shampooing as normal.

If your hair is dull, try mixing equal amounts of lemon juice and warm olive oil. Towel dry your hair then massage the oil and lemon mixture into your scalp. Wrap a towel round your head and leave it for an hour before shampooing as normal.

For damaged hair, try making your own hot oil treatment. Heat a little olive or vegetable oil by pouring it into an egg cup and standing it in a small bowl of very hot water for five minutes. Massage the oil into your hair, making sure to cover the ends, then leave for 30 minutes. Rinse well.

For another great conditioning treatment, massage natural yoghurt into your hair, and leave for 15 minutes before rinsing.

# FACEMASKS

**Different skin types need different masks, so try these to find which is best for you.**

Spread whole egg mayonnaise on your face and leave for 15 minutes for a great conditioning mask.

Mash a very ripe banana with some honey, spread it on your face and leave it for 15 minutes before rinsing really well.

For clogged pores, mash some cucumber and spread it over the skin. Leave for ten minutes before rinsing with lukewarm water and dabbing with toner.

# TEN TOP TIPS

**And finally, follow these tips to look and feel great at all times.**

**1.** Drink lots of water every day.
**2.** For fresh breath, chew a sprig of parsley.
**3.** Once a week, scrub your body with a handful of sea-salt to remove dead skin.
**4.** Use Vaseline (petroleum jelly) instead of hand cream.
**5.** Yoghurt is great for soothing sunburn.
**6.** Rub olive oil into your eyelashes to make them look lush and long.
**7.** Soften rough feet and hands by scrubbing with a mixture of cooking oil and sugar!
**8.** Soften cuticles on finger and toenails by soaking them in castor oil.
**9.** Spread Vaseline on your lips before you go to bed to keep them soft and plump.
**10.** For great hair conditioning, add a capful of fabric conditioner to your final rinse.

# it's a

## SOME WEIRD 'N' WACKY FACTS FROM THE ANIMAL WORLD.

- *Rats can't be sick!*

- *A goldfish has a memory span of three seconds!*

- *Polar bears are left-handed! Dogs, however, are like humans and can favour either left or right side!*

- Domestic cats spend around 70% of each day sleeping!

- *A rat can last longer without water than a camel!*

- Lobsters have blue blood!

- *Ants don't sleep!*

- The chow is the only dog without a pink tongue. His is black!

- Pigs always need to have shelter cos they can burn in the sun!

- *A bird eats more food in proportion to its size than a baby!*

- The fastest bird is the spine-tailed swift. It can fly at speeds of up to **220** miles an hour!

- Giraffes can be more than six feet tall at birth!

- *Butterflies taste with their feet!*

- Mosquitos kill more humans than any other animal - and bees kill more people than poisonous snakes do.

- Zebras are white with black stripes!

# Fact...

- **The fastest snail travels at 0.0313 miles per hour!**

- Elephants are the only animals that can't jump!

- The world's largest mammal, the blue whale, can weigh 50 tons at birth!

- **It takes 40 minutes to hard boil an ostrich egg!**

- A lion's roar can be heard up to five miles away!

- Tigers have striped skin as well as striped fur!

- Snakes cannot poison themselves!

- **No two spiders' webs are the same!**

- Moles can tunnel through 300 feet of earth in a day!

- **Goldfish loose their colour when they're in running water!**

- **The most popular names for dogs are Sam for boys and Trixie for girls!**

## Paws For Thought!

Unscramble the letters to find four popular dog breeds.

**PNGSRIRE NEPAISL**

**MRNGAE DPEHSEHR**

**KSRIYROHE REITRER**

**LNOGED EVERRITER**

## Cracking Chat!

From the letters given, can you crack the code to find out what the bird is saying?

Code:
A is represented by C, C by I, E by O, R by B, S by E  etc

*Tip. Write out the whole alphabet, filling in the letters you know. The sequence should soon become clear.*

FSFFW'E C VBOHHW FSW

## Piggy in the Middle!

Fit the name of one of the pets listed into each set of brackets to make ten new words or phrases.
eg BLACK (RAT) TRAP
Which pet isn't used?

bird fish mouse
horse cat dog

GOLD (    ) PIE
HOT (    ) ROSE
COOL (    ) NAP
BLACK (    ) BRAIN
SEA (    ) BOX

## Spot the Differences!

These two pictures look exactly the same, but there are five differences. Can you spot them?

# Puzzles!

## All Square!

Score out the letters that appear more than once in each square. The remaining letters, when rearranged, will spell out the names of two popular pets.

**DRAP**
**VTLD**
**MVPS**
**EPHL**

**SNCE**
**ABRG**
**HGNA**
**NCOB**

## Dig Deep!

Lead the rabbit family to the centre of their burrow.

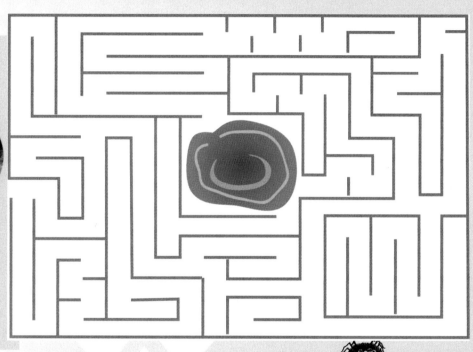

## Yikes!

How many itsy bitsy spiders can you see on these pages?

# You will need...

A selection of different sized cardboard tubes from kitchen-rolls, toilet-rolls etc
Thin card or thick paper
A silver or gold cake base
Glue
Sticky tape
Craft paint
Paint brush
Scissors
Tinsel and gold or silver foil to decorate

● Decide which towers you want to have battlements, then carefully cut out notches all the way round the top of the cardboard tube.

● Paint the outside *and* inside of the tubes using the craft paint, then leave them to dry.  Depending on the colour you choose, you may have to give everything more than one coat.

100 mm

Glue here

85 mm

7 mm

● To make the turrets, use this template to help you cut out shapes from paper or card. Stick together as shown and then, when the glue is dry, paint the turrets to match your castle.

*This size, when assembled, makes a turret to fit an average toilet-roll tube.*

# Upon A Time...

These fairytale castles make beautiful and unusual Christmas decorations - and, believe it or not, they're really easy to make. So get busy and wow your friends this Chrimbo.

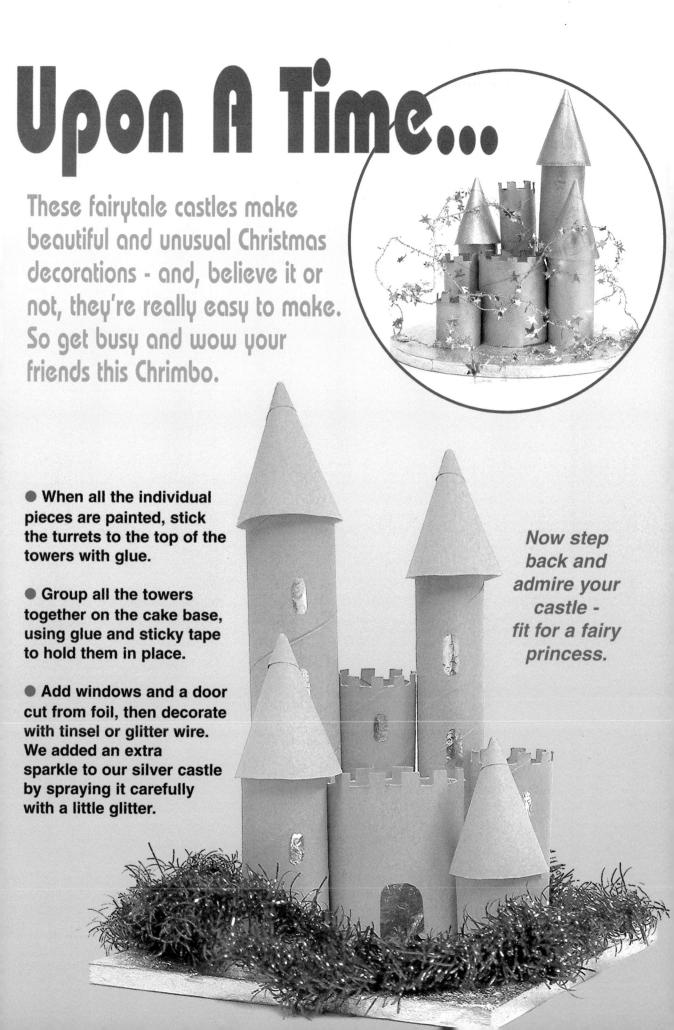

● When all the individual pieces are painted, stick the turrets to the top of the towers with glue.

● Group all the towers together on the cake base, using glue and sticky tape to hold them in place.

● Add windows and a door cut from foil, then decorate with tinsel or glitter wire. We added an extra sparkle to our silver castle by spraying it carefully with a little glitter.

*Now step back and admire your castle - fit for a fairy princess.*

Best
Friends

# Surprise!

KELLY and Lauren had lived next door to each other for years and, although Kelly was a year older, the two were good friends. Kelly was going to her gran's for a holiday —

Two whole weeks, Kelly. I'll really miss you.

And I'll miss *you*, Lauren. But I'm looking forward to going away, too. I haven't seen Gran for ages.

Promise you'll text me every day? And phone? And write?

I'll try. But I'm going to be dead busy.

But please, Kel. You're my best friend and I'll be really lonely while you're away.

Okay, Lauren. I promise to get in touch as often as I can. That's all I can say.

Phew! Lauren's a good mate, but she can be tough going at times. I just wish she would make some other friends, too. Then she might not be so clingy.

Well, I'll do what I promised and keep in touch — but I'm not going to let Lauren ruin my holiday.

And —

Here you are at last! Oh, it's so good to see you all.

And you, Mum.

Little Kelly! I'd hardly have recognised you. You've grown so much since I last saw you. And you're so pretty.

Thanks, Gran. I must take after you.

This is your room, love. I hope it's okay.

It's lovely. I'll just unpack and then come downstairs.

But first I'll text Lauren to tell her we've arrived. That'll keep her happy.

*For the next two days Kelly relaxed, then —*

These are cute cards. I'll buy one to send to Lauren instead of a postcard.

*And later —*

Hi. Posting a letter back home?

Yeah. To my friend.

I've just sent a card to my little sister. I'm Alex by the way.

Hi, I'm Kelly. I'm staying at my gran's nearby.

Oh, I'm staying with my aunt for a holiday. My sister had to stay at home in Hilton cos she hurt her foot.

Look, I don't know anyone else here, so do you fancy going swimming or something? It's not much fun on my own.

Hilton? Really? I'm from Bagsworth. That's only about five miles away from you.

That's amazing! What a coincidence.

Yeah okay.

Alex is really nice. Friendly, too.

68

So —

I really am enjoying this — and I really like Alex, too. I don't have this much fun with Lauren.

Phew! I'm shattered. That was worse than helping with the little ones at school. Talking of which, what school do you go to?

Hilton Junior. But I'm moving up to Shelby High after the holidays.

Really? So am I. We'll be able to chum up there, too.

Brilliant! We can meet before that, though. I'll come to visit you, or you can come over to Hilton.

There's my mobile number. We're off home tomorrow but, if you call me next week, we can arrange something.

Sure will. I never thought I'd make a new school friend when I came here on holiday.

Next day, when Kelly arrived home —

I suppose I'd better go round and see Lauren. I thought she'd be at the door to meet us when we got back, but there's no sign. She's obviously still huffing with me.

But —

She's not in, Kelly. She's visiting a friend and won't be back till later.

Okay. Thanks, Mrs Gray.

A friend? Wow, that's new! But I'm glad.

# SISTERS

## A sister is someone who...

...puts herself through all sorts of torture in the hope of becoming beautiful...

...doesn't eat cakes and puddings cos they'll make her fat – but can eat a whole box of chocs when her boyfriend dumps her...

...spends hours chatting to friends on the phone – just when *you* want to make a call...

...hates walking, but will go miles out of her way to pass 'his' house...

...can't do the washing-up in case it ruins her nails...

...moans about being treated like a child, yet still takes her cuddly toy to bed...

...is great when you need to borrow clothes – especially when she doesn't know you're doing it!

## And that's why we love 'em!

73

Almost everyone has, at one time or another, owned and loved a Teddy Bear. But do you know when they first appeared? And how they got their name? If not, then you're about to find out!

# THE Bea

learning to be a dressmaker and opening a shop selling soft goods made from felt. In 1880 the only children's toys Margarete supplied were little felt elephants, but monkeys, donkeys, camels and other types of animals soon followed – along with a successful mail-order business. This marked the beginning of toy manufacturing as we know it.

As the business grew, Margarete's three eldest nephews, Richard, Paul and Franz, entered the business. Then, in 1902, Richard designed the first jointed bear, and Teddy, as we know him today, was born.

## THE HISTORY

The most famous toy bears are made by a German company, which was founded by a remarkable woman called Margarete Steiff.

Shortly after she was born in 1847, Margarete became ill with polio and, for the rest of her life, was confined to a wheelchair. But Margarete was a brave and determined woman and her disability didn't stop her from

## WHAT'S IN A NAME...?

But how did Teddy get his name? Well, the most popular story says that, while on a shooting trip in 1902, US president, Theodore (Teddy) Roosevelt, refused to shoot a young bear which had been previously captured and tied to a tree.

The next day a newspaper showed a cartoon of the incident and, when it was spotted by a shopkeeper, Morris Michtom, he decided to display two toy bears in his New York shop

1880    2005

# r Facts!

window. The bears, which had been made by Michtom's wife, Rose, were immediately popular, so Morris asked permission from Roosevelt to call them "Teddy's Bears".
The president agreed and the little stuffed bears were a huge success – becoming known as Teddy Bears all over the world.

OR...

One other legend is that President Roosevelt was attending a large dinner where the tables were decorated with bears, most of which were dressed as hunters or fishermen in honour of the president. When someone asked what breed of bear they were, another guest laughed and said, "Teddy Bears, of course!".

So there you have it. Take your pick as to which story you like best – or ask your Teddy to decide!

*The limited edition "Celebration Bear" shown here was produced to mark 125 years of the Steiff company.*
*Steiff products are available in the Steiff Galleries, in specialist toy retailers, in the toy sections of department stores, on the Internet and in the new "Die Welt von Steiff" (World of Steiff) museum, which can be found at the company's grounds in Giengen an der Brenz, Germany.*

## Did you know...

● *Teddy Bear collecting is big business! Teddy Bear shows and jamborees are held all over the world, and there are even special Teddy Bear magazines available.*

● *Famous Teddy Bears include Winnie the Pooh, Paddington Bear, Rupert and, of course, The Three Bears.*

● *Teddy Bears can fetch huge prices at auction. In 1994 a Steiff Teddy Girl was sold for £100, 000.*

● *There are lots of songs about Teddy Bears - one of the most famous being The Teddy Bears' Picnic which was written in 1993.*

● *Around 40% of adults still own the Teddy Bear they had as a child.*

● *Teddy Bears have always been popular gifts- and not just for children. Many adults carry small Teddy Bear mascots in the hope that they'll bring them luck.*

1880  2005

# All About...KEIRA

- Keira Knightley was born in Teddington, Middlesex, on March 22, 1985. This means she is a Pisces person.

- Keira showed an interest in acting from a young age. It's said that she asked her parents to find her an agent when she was three.

- Keira trained as a dancer when she was young.

- Keira's first film role was when she was nine years old.

- She has one brother, Caleb, who was born in 1979.

- Her first big role was in the hit football comedy 'Bend it Like Beckham'.

- While she was at school, Keira's parents would only let her work in the holidays – and only then if it didn't interfere with her homework.

- One of her worst moments was in 'Pirates of the Caribbean', when she had to walk the plank. It wobbled around a lot and made her feel very dizzy.

- The actresses Keira most admires are old style Hollywood stars, such as Katharine Hepburn and Vivien Leigh.

- Keira left school at 16.

- When it comes to real life football, Keira supports West Ham United.

- When asked what it was like to kiss Orlando Bloom she said, "Lovely!".

- Starring roles to date have included such wonderful characters as Lara in 'Doctor Zhivago', Guinevere in 'King Arthur' and Elizabeth Bennet in 'Pride and Prejudice'.

- Keira was born into a show business family. Her father, Will, is an actor and her mother is a playwright.

- She has described herself as 'a bit of a tomboy'.

- In 2004, Keira moved into a flat with six friends. She was the only actor amongst the girls.

# Cinderella Jones

I might just be able to squeeze you in on the top floor, Mrs Prendegast, but I'm afraid my prices are up on last year's.

*C*INDY JONES worked hard for her keep at the Happyholme Guest House, Brightsea, which was owned by her stepmother. Cindy's stepsisters, Isobelle and Sarah, did nothing to help.

Stepmother loves Christmas. It just means more money for her!

*Just then Claude, Isobelle's husband, arrived —*

Here we are, Mrs J. Last year's Christmas tree — as good as new!

He's just dug it up from the garden!

Set it up in the corner, Claude.

Look at my clean floor!

Stepmother is a real Scrooge. She's even got Isobelle and Sarah making the Christmas decorations.

Make us some more paste, Cindy!

Yes! And quickly!

*Cindy's father was a sales rep and, that evening —*

Dad! So you managed to get time off this weekend, after all!

I'm afraid so, Cindy — lots of it.

I've been made redundant!

Oh, Dad, that's awful! So near to Christmas, too!

Out of work, are you? Well, you needn't think you're going to laze around here all day doing nothing, Arnold Jones! You can start helping by tidying up the cellar!

*There were lots of other jobs for Mr Jones to do, too —*

And when you've finished that you can scrub the floor.

How's it going, Dad? I've brought you some tea.

Put your back into it, Arnold! There's the attic to start on next!

Yes, dear.

Poor Dad! Stepmother hasn't given him a moment's rest since he arrived!

*Later —*

You're missing the corners, Arnold! If a job's worth doing, it's worth doing properly!

Yes, dear!

Yes, dear. No, dear! Why does Dad put up with it?

Why don't you stand up to her, Dad? Show her who's boss for a change!

Oh, you know me, Cindy — anything for a quiet life. Besides, it's only right I should earn my keep!

There, the tree's finished, Mother! Claude's just putting the fairy on the top.

Yes, fairy on top.

Very nice, girls.

I've swept the drive, Agnes. What do you want me to do next?

Aaaagh!!

Careful, Dad . . .

You can clear up this mess and put the tree back to rights, you great useless pudding!

You've ruined *everything* — and after all our hard work, too!

Yes, all our hard work.

That evening, Cindy met her old friend, Charlie Prince —

Dad's so quiet, Charlie, he just lets Stepmother walk all over him! I wish, just once, he'd put her in her place!

I'd like to help, Cindy, but I just don't see there's anything I can do.

Next morning —

The postman's early this morning . . . and this letter's open.

**The next day —**

There's a letter here for you, Arnold. It might be your redundancy cheque! I'll open it.

Very well, dear.

It's probably just junk mail, but . . . wait a minute! Now this is *very* interesting!

It's from the Tourist Board! It says Happyholme is in the running for their Gold Star Leisure Award! A rep, Mr Rudge, will be visiting to make an assessment!

If we are awarded the Gold Star, we'll be able to charge more!

I wonder why the letter was addressed to me.

Probably they expect the man of the house to be in charge, Dad.

**Two days later —**

Mr Jones? I'm Alfred Rudge from the Tourist Board. You got my letter?

Yes, come right in, Mr Rudge.

Let's get rid of the apron, Dad!

May I take your hat and coat, sir?

Certainly, my dear. Glad to see you've got your staff on the mark, Jones! I like to see a proprietor who's clearly in charge of the ship!

Er — yes, of course. I-I'd like you to meet my wife, Agnes.

Actually, it's Agnes who's . .

Pleased to meet you, Mr Rudge. Oh, my husband runs Happyholme like a well-oiled machine!

I'll start my assessment by sampling the food, Jones!

You should tell them you *you're* the boss, Agnes.

Keep quiet! If it means us winning the gold award, he's welcome to think you're boss!

My wife does all the cooking. I insist on it!

Nothing like homemade soup, eh? Oops! Dropped my spoon!

Fetch Mr Rudge a clean spoon, my dear. and be quick about it. We don't want his soup going cold!

Yes, dear.

Later —

You see, Mr Rudge, Happyholme is very much a family concern. I insist on all the family taking a share of the chores.

As it should be, Jones!

Tut, tut! Is this grease I see, Agnes? I think we'd better wash these plates again!

Of course, Arnold — just as you say!

The speed in which a room is cleaned is vitally important, Jones.

I can assure you, my staff is really on the ball when it comes to making beds, sir. All right, girls, let's move it for Mr Rudge!

I'm impressed, Jones. You'll be receiving the results in a few days' time.

Glad to be of service, Mr Rudge! Agnes — Mr Rudge's hat and coat! Lively now!

Well, how did I do, Agnes?

Very well, Arnold — but just don't push your luck!

Oh, boy! I enjoyed that!

*On Christmas Eve —*

It's from the Tourist Board, Agnes! Happyholme has been awarded the Gold Star!

So Mr Rudge liked what he saw!

It's no more than we deserve, of course.

Cindy, I can't help feeling I've seen that Mr Rudge before. And this letter from the Tourist Board — it's more than a week old!

Ah, yes — well maybe I can explain, Dad.

Happyholme was granted the Gold Award because of residents' recommendations. The letter arrived last week and sort of came unstuck.

Charlie asked his actor cousin to play the part of Mr Rudge. I thought it was time you were given a chance to assert yourself. I hope you're not angry.

*Angry!* This is the best Christmas present I've ever had!

Happy Christmas, everyone!

Yes, happy Christmas!

THE END

82

# MEET ME!

**OR IN THIS CASE, MEET US!**

We're Sophie and Katie Kelly and, just in case you hadn't noticed, we're identical twins. In fact, the only **sure** way to tell us apart is to look down our throats. Why? It's simple. Sophie has tonsils and Katie doesn't.

When Katie was in hospital having her tonsils out we played a trick on the nurse. One visiting time we swapped places and fooled everyone. The nurse even gave the wrong twin the medicine - which wasn't quite so funny for Sophie.

There are other differences between us - but not ones anyone would notice. For example, Sophie likes carrots and chocolate cake, while Katie turns up her nose at both. We both sing and dance, too, but Sophie is the stronger singer, while Katie is a slightly better ballerina.

We love looking so much alike cos it seems to make us very popular. People are always coming up to us and asking which is which. We make lots of friends that way.

Unlike some twins, we **like** dressing the same and we even have the same best friend. We choose to share a bedroom, too, so instead of a room each we have one bedroom and one 'playroom'. That's where we keep all our 'treasures' - so come on in and take a look.

**Katie cuddles up to her toy cat...**   **...while Sophie shows off her 'S' bear.**

This is our 'achievements' wall. It holds all the certificates and awards we have won for singing and dancing.

These fluffy fairy lights show off our TV and music centre.

This computer was bought to help us with our homework.

What a double act! Sophie plays the guitar, while Katie hits the keyboard.

Mum buys us a little bear every time we win a dancing badge. As you can see, we've got quite a few.

I love joining in with Whitney Huston, while Katie dances to Motown sounds.

My favourite author is Jacqueline Wilson, and Sophie likes Mary Kate and Ashley books.

And we're in perfect harmony behind a microphone.

We were given these matching star-shaped 'bear' pillows at Christmas. We added our favourite fairy lights later.

So that's it. It's time for us to get ready for another dancing event, but we hope you've enjoyed meeting us and hearing about a few of our favourite things.

# PUZZLE TIME!

## Two pages of tricky teasers!

### Be A Sport!

A simple one to start. Name all the sports stars pictured here.

b

c

## Trace the Place!

| E | A | M | A | I | S | I | U |
|---|---|---|---|---|---|---|---|
| N | I | A | N | I | S | L | O |
| L | L | I | N | O | D | I | A |
| I | O | I | O | H | A | I | D |
| E | X | H | O | M | A | R | O |
| T | A | S | O | O | N | F | L |
| A | K | S | K | H | E | K | R |
| A | L | A | L | A | W | Y | O |

Starting in one of the corner squares, make your way through the grid, finding the names of **ten** US States. You can travel up, down and across, but **not** diagonally, and no letter is used more than once. We've given you a list of twelve states. Which are **not** used?

| | |
|---|---|
| **Alaska** | **Maine** |
| **California** | **Nevada** |
| **Florida** | **NewYork** |
| **Idaho** | **Ohio** |
| **Illinois** | **Oklahoma** |
| **Louisiana** | **Texas** |

# True or False!

As simple as it sounds.  Which of these star statements are true, and which are false?

**a)** Avril used to sing in a church choir.
**b)** Atomic Kitten used to be known as Nuclear Cat.
**c)** Britney's middle name is Joan.
**d)** Hilary Duff has a sister called Haylie.
**e)** Natasha Bedingfield is Daniel's big sister.

# Star Spotting!

The peeps shown here are all TV stars - although this isn't how you usually see them.  Can you name them and the shows they appear in?

# All Mixed Up!

The names of four European countries have been jumbled up.  Can you unscramble the letters to find the countries then, for an extra point, name the capital cities of each.

**a)** AROPGULT

**c)** MEILBUG

**b)** TAYIL

**d)** URAISAT

# The Frog Prince

Clean? You call this clean? Do it again, wretch!

ONCE upon a time, many years ago, Lady Eleanor Fontaine lived with her father, Lord Hugo, in their fine castle. But although Eleanor was the most beautiful girl in the kingdom, she was also vain and cold-hearted —

But, Lady Eleanor, I've done it twice already.

Don't argue with me, girl, or I shall instruct my father to send you packing.

Although she was known to have a cruel temper, Eleanor was so pretty that she had no shortage of suitors —

My lord, I would like your permission to marry your daughter. In the future.

My dear young fellow, as far as *I'm* concerned, you can marry her today. But, frankly, I doubt that she'll have you!

But he's the eldest son of a baron, Eleanor. His father owns half the county!

A baron? I shall not marry until I find a *prince!* I am too beautiful to waste myself on a baron's son!

*And, soon —*

His Royal Highness, the Prince of Danubia!

A prince at last. For goodness sake, try to be charming, Eleanor!

I'm *always* charming, Father!

*But —*

. . . and as well as every-day servants, I shall require a personal trainer, a stylist, two chefs — preferably celebrities — and . . .

My thanks for your hospitality, my lord, but I must return to Danubia unexpectedly.

Pray do not apologise, my boy. I quite understand.

*Time passed, and Lord Hugo began to despair of Eleanor ever marrying. Then, one Christmas —*

Go and distribute these gold pieces to the poor children of the village, Eleanor. It is a tradition.

Tch! What a waste, giving gold to those ragamuffins! But, if you insist, Father.

90

# go with

## What's the creative job for you?
## Follow our fun flowchart to find out.

**START**

**Are you good at English at school?**

**When walking, do you often stop to admire things like flowers and views?**

**Is art your all time favourite school subject?**

**Do your friends come to you for advice on clothes and make up?**

**Do you enjoy listening in to other people's conversations?**

**Do you think you talk too much?**

**Do you get bored when you're on your own?**

**You always get invited to the coolest parties. True?**

**You love experimenting with make up. True?**

# the flow!

**Do you usually have a good memory?**

— N → **Would you rather draw something than use words to describe it?**

— Y → **You prefer to read magazines rather than books. True?**

— Y → **ARTIST –**

You have a flair for colour and design and enjoy looking at all the beautiful things around you. You don't always have to be part of a crowd and love drawing and painting, so you'd be a superb artist.

**WRITER –**

You're quite nosy and have lots of imagination, but you don't like a lot of noise and fuss. You really enjoy juggling with words and, as you very seldom get bored when on your own, you'd make an ideal writer.

**Do you enjoy working in a team?**

**Your favourite parties are fancy dress. True?**

**Do words sometimes confuse you?**

**Would you like to appear on television?**

**Do you like to be the centre of attention?**

**ACTRESS –**

You like words and enjoy working with lots of other people, so you'd make a terrific actress. You're also bright, chatty, noisy and love experimenting with make up and dressing up – a natural star in fact.

# Happy BirthdAy!

**P**HOEBE looked at the calendar. Just a few more days, and then she'd be three. Well, actually, she'd be twelve but, as she had been born on the 29th of February, it would be her third real birthday. She just knew everyone would start making jokes — and at least four people were sure to give her cards saying "3 years old Today", just like they had done on her 'second' birthday. Still, at least Mum had said she could invite her friends to a day out at the nearby pottery. You were allowed to join in and make your own mugs and stuff there, so that was something to look forward to.

"I've invited one other person," said Mum later that day. "You remember Elle, Sally Lester's daughter?"

"Oh, no, not her," Phoebe gasped! "I can't stand her."

"But her mother's ill, and I said Elle could come and stay for a day or so. Please say you don't mind," Mum smiled, hopefully.

"But I **do** mind!" Phoebe snapped. "She's awful. She says I'm a baby, just because I look younger than her. She's sure to make stupid jokes about me being a three-year-old toddler."

"Oh, please, Phoebe," Mum pleaded. "I can't let Sally down."

So, on the Saturday before her birthday, Phoebe found herself sitting at the pottery table — right next to Elle. She tried to concentrate on the pink flowers she was painting on her dish, but her eyes kept drifting over to Elle, who was staring at the lop-sided mug she was supposed to decorate.

Every so often one of the girls would get up and walk around the table to look at everyone else's work. As Elle stopped to look at Phoebe's dish, she wrinkled her nose.

"What's that supposed to be?" she asked, as she leaned forward to pick it up.

"None of your business," Phoebe snapped, stretching out to grab her dish. But she was too late. The dish rocked between the two girls, fell to the floor and smashed. Phoebe's flowers lay on the floor, broken into tiny pieces.

Phoebe was furious. But, suddenly, Mum's mobile phone went, and Elle turned white. Phoebe couldn't fail to notice the look of fear in the girl's eyes as she followed Mum out to the corridor.

A hush went round the table as all the girls sensed that something important was going on. Even Phoebe's best friend, Millie, stopped chattering and concentrated on the pattern she was painting.

Then, about five minutes later, Elle and Phoebe's mum came back. Mum was smiling and had her arm round Elle. The girl was smiling, too, but it was obvious that she had been crying. They both came over to Phoebe.

"That was Elle's mum on the phone," Mum said quietly. "She's been in hospital for an operation — but everything's gone well and she's going to be okay."

"I'm really sorry I broke your dish," Phoebe said. "And that I was nasty about it. I was just jealous because it was so much nicer than my mug. And — and I was worried about Mum, too."

"That's okay," Phoebe said kindly. "I understand. I'll paint another dish for you to give to your mum, if you like. I'm really glad she's going to be okay."

Millie heard all the details from Phoebe at school on Monday.

"You know, I was wrong about Elle. She's really nice underneath."

"It was still a bit mean of her to tease you about looking young — **and** to smash your dish," said Millie.

"But she didn't mean to break the dish," explained Phoebe. "And she says she wishes she looked young — just like me."

"That was nice of her," said Millie. "And I don't see you wearing a '3 Today' badge, so she obviously didn't give you one."

"No," smiled Phoebe. "Nobody did! Everyone's given me really nice cards."

"Until now," giggled Millie as she handed over a bulky, bright yellow envelope. "You know I always like to be original."

Phoebe knew what was inside before she opened the envelope. But, strangely, she didn't mind any more. And when she pinned the badge with the words "Happy Birthday 3 Today" on to her jumper, she felt special, not silly.

"Happy Birthday," said Millie with a teasing grin. "What does it feel like to be a toddler?"

The End

Best Friends

# The Ghost Walk

ONE sunny morning last summer, somewhere in the north of England —

What a great day for a walk! I just love these warm summer days.

Let's see. Armley Fell is where I want to go, I think.

MOORTON FELL    ARMLEY FELL

Just then —

Hey! Stop!

Oh! I wonder what those hikers want!

I wouldn't recommend going that way. That path leads to Armley Fell.

I know. That's where I want to go.

THE END

# MERRY CHRISTMAS!

*Get some festive spirit with this cool Christmas wordsearch.*

**The 46 festive things listed here are hidden in the square. Can you find them all? Words can read forwards, backwards, up, down or diagonally and letters can be used more than once.**

## HAVE FUN!

| balloons | bells |
|---|---|
| bows | breadsauce |
| cake | candles |
| cards | carols |
| chestnuts | chocolates |
| crackers | cranberries |
| dates | decorations |
| elves | fairylights |
| frankincense | frosty |
| garlands | glitter |
| gold | holly |
| ice cream | ivy |
| mince pies | mints |
| mistletoe | myrrh |
| pantomime | parties |
| plum pudding | presents |
| reindeer | robin |
| rudolph | santa |
| skating | sleighride |
| snow | star |
| stocking | tangerines |
| tinsel | tree |
| turkey | wrapping paper |

| G | W | S | E | I | P | E | C | N | I | M | O | T | R | E | E | I | G |
|---|---|---|---|---|---|---|---|---|---|---|---|---|---|---|---|---|---|
| A | B | L | M | F | N | Y | H | P | S | Y | Z | D | O | K | Q | N | E |
| R | S | E | I | R | R | E | B | N | A | R | C | N | A | S | I | E | M |
| L | L | I | M | E | E | A | C | I | N | R | Z | C | T | T | N | A | S |
| A | L | G | O | T | P | N | N | U | T | H | G | N | A | C | E | D | B |
| N | E | H | T | T | A | J | Q | K | A | N | E | K | R | R | R | S | T |
| D | B | R | N | I | P | Z | I | S | I | S | S | U | C | A | O | D | I |
| S | E | I | A | L | G | J | R | D | E | N | D | E | C | C | B | L | N |
| T | Z | D | P | G | N | E | D | R | O | O | C | A | S | K | I | O | S |
| H | F | E | Y | C | I | U | P | O | L | I | S | E | E | E | N | G | E |
| G | L | O | G | N | P | E | L | P | H | T | T | E | N | R | V | Q | L |
| I | S | T | D | M | P | L | H | J | O | A | N | V | I | S | B | L | V |
| L | G | E | U | L | A | F | B | C | L | R | I | R | R | T | E | C | E |
| Y | E | L | L | B | R | S | K | O | L | O | M | Y | E | K | R | U | T |
| R | P | T | X | D | W | I | C | O | Y | C | S | M | G | O | A | A | I |
| I | G | S | M | O | N | O | V | C | H | E | S | T | N | U | T | S | P |
| A | W | I | B | G | H | A | N | Y | M | D | U | E | A | C | S | H | G |
| F | Y | M | P | C | Y | T | C | S | V | J | V | Y | T | S | O | R | F |

# Odd One Out

CLAIRE WARD and her friends always met up in the town on Saturday afternoon —

Where do you fancy going first? You choose this week, Rachel.

Okay, I . . . oh!

That's Dave Bremner, isn't it? He's waving to you, Rachel.

I know. I mentioned I'd be here, but I wasn't sure if he'd turn up.

I-I'll catch up with you later, girls.

Oh, yeah? Bet you don't!

Lucky old Rachel. Dave's gorgeous.

Huh! So much for our Saturday shopping, though!

But we go shopping *every* week. Spending an afternoon with a boy is something special.

Yeah! I don't blame her a bit!

And later, in the cafe —

Huh! Now Sarah's sitting with Andy Todd. You're not about to clear off with a boyfriend are you, Amy?

Loosen up, Claire. Sarah's just enjoying herself.

I'll wait here, girls. Andy's mum's coming for him so I'll get home with them.

Okay, Sarah. See you.

D'you mind popping into the corner shop before we go home? There's something I want to check out.

No probs. It's on the way to the bus stop, anyway.

But —

Tom! I forgot you worked here on a Saturday!

Forgot? Huh! That's a good one. I bet the only thing she wanted to check out was Tom!

Well, she needn't expect me to hang around playing gooseberry. I'm off home.

We used to stick together, but I guess the others are more interested in boyfriend's now. That leaves me the odd one out. I've never had a boyfriend!

But then I . . .

ohhhhhh!

Hey, look out!

Oh, it's you, Claire. I thought I was being mugged for a minute! You were certainly lost in thought.

Oh — oh, yes Paul.

Of all the people to bump into, I choose Paul Denton — the lower school pin-up!

D'you wanna talk about what's bothering you? We could go for a Coke if you like.

I-I'd better not, Paul. I want to catch the four o'clock bus.

I don't believe I actually said that. He'll think I'm a half wit!

But —

I'll walk you to your stop, then. We can chat on the way.

Claire found Paul very easy to talk to —

. . . so now I'm on my own!

Something similar happened to me! My mates sent a text to say they'd been given tickets for the footie. That left me high and dry. It's a pity we hadn't met up earlier.

But what about meeting up later? We could go to the cinema.

That would be really good! Thanks, Paul.

Okay, then. I'll see you outside the cinema at seven.

I don't believe this is happening to me!

I must be one of the luckiest girls around. The others'll be dead jealous!

And later —

That was great, wasn't it? I love those sci-fi movies.

Mmm! Er — me too.

To be honest, it was a real bore — but I'd better not say anything.

On Monday —

Is Paul as nice as he looks?

Tell all, Claire.

Has he asked you out, again?

106

Yeah and yeah!

I won't say anything about the film being a bore. That might spoil things.

...Claire and Paul met up regularly —

Then —

Do you want to come over tonight, Claire? The other girls will all be here?

I can't, Amy. i said I would go round to Paul's.

Oh, well. Some other time perhaps.

Yeah!

We haven't met up for ages, and it would have been fun. But I suppose Paul has to come first.

Later —

This is the new game I got. I've already worked my way to level 13. Aren't the graphics cool?

Yeah, I guess so.

107

Paul's really into these games. I may as well not be here.

Then, on Friday night —

Oh, there are the girls. Funny. I thought they'd be out with their boyfriends.

Hi. You never said you were having a girls' night out!

Well, you told us you were meeting Paul, so there wasn't any point in mentioning it.

We're going to see the new romantic comedy at the multi-cinema. It's supposed to be great. Are you going?

No way! That's a chick flick. We're off to 'Revenge of the Killer Robots'.

Which sounds thrilling — not!

But what about your boyfriends? Aren't you meeting Dave? Or Andy and Tom?

Tch! Dave turned out to be a bore. He only likes football and computer games.

And Andy's never been my boyfriend, just my next door neighbour. We're mates, nothing more.

But what about you, Amy? You're always chatting to Tom, so you must fancy him.

THE END

# BROTHERS
## A brother is someone who...

...never gets up before noon when it's not a school day...

...spends hours combing his hair in front of mirrors and shop windows...

...plays his CDs and tapes all the time – even when he's asleep...

...wears his jacket two sizes too big to make him look as if he's got super-broad shoulders...

...gets kicked to pieces on the football field without complaining, then cries like a baby when he gets a splinter in his finger...

...spends even more time in the bathroom than you do...

...has lots of gorgeous mates for you to drool over!

**And that's why we love 'em!**

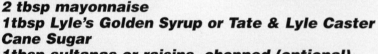

## SUMMERTiME DiP
**(Serves 6)**
**Ingredients:**
**1 crisp eating apple**
**100g cream cheese**
**1-2 tbsp tomato sauce**
**2 tbsp mayonnaise**
**1tbsp Lyle's Golden Syrup or Tate & Lyle Caster Cane Sugar**
**1tbsp sultanas or raisins, chopped (optional)**
**1tbsp orange or lemon juice**

### Method
1. Peel, core and grate the apple into a large bowl.

2. Add all other ingredients to the apple and beat vigorously with a wooden spoon until creamy.

3. Pour the dip into a small dish and leave for an hour to chill.  Serve with bite-sized pieces of prepared vegetables such as celery, pepper, cucumber and carrot.

**PURE CANE SUGAR**

**Impress your friends and family with these delicious summer-time treats from Tate and Lyle.**

### OVER THE RAiNBOW
**(Serves 8)**
**Ingredients:**
*Orange Jelly*
**3 tbsp hot water**
**1 sachet of powdered gelatine**
**300ml unsweetened orange juice**
**Approx 25g Tate & Lyle Caster Cane Sugar, to taste**

*Green Jelly*
**3 tbsp hot water**
**1 sachet of powdered gelatine**
**300ml strong lime juice**
**Tate & Lyle Caster Cane Sugar, to taste**

*Red Jelly*
**3 tbsp hot water**
**1 sachet of powdered gelatine**
**300ml cranberry juice**
**Tate & Lyle Caster Cane Sugar, to taste**

### Method:
1. Make each of the individual jellies by putting the hot water into a bowl and sprinkling on the gelatine. Leave for five to ten minutes to dissolve, then stir well.

# lers!

### STRAWBERRY & APPLE FOAM
**(Serves 8)**
**Ingredients:**
**225g strawberries (or raspberries or blackberries)**
**450g Bramley cooking apples, peeled, cored and thinly sliced**
**100g Tate & Lyle Light Brown Soft Cane Sugar**
**25g butter or margarine**
**2 tbsp water**
**170g can evaporated milk, well chilled**
**1 lemon jelly**

**Method:**
**1.** Remove the green stalks from the centre of the strawberries. Put eight berries aside, and place the remainder into a large saucepan with a close fitting lid.

**2.** Add the apples, sugar, butter and water to the saucepan, replace the lid and simmer until the fruit is mushy (about 15 minutes). Leave to cool slightly.

**3.** Strain the stewed fruit through a sieve, pouring the liquid into a measuring jug. Add water to make the liquid up to 450ml.

**4.** Pour the liquid into the washed saucepan, bring to the boil them remove from the heat and add the jelly cubes. Stir until melted, then leave until cool.

**5.** Whisk the evaporated milk until it becomes thick, frothy, and doubles in size.

**6.** Chop the reserved strawberries and add half of them to the cooled jelly and fruit juice. Gently stir in the whisked evaporated milk, then spoon the mixture into individual glasses or bowls.

**7.** Leave to set in the fridge, then decorate with the remaining strawberries and some sprigs of mint.

**2.** Pour one mix of gelatine and water into the orange juice. Add sugar to taste, then heat the juice in a saucepan over a gentle heat until the liquid is warm. Remove from the heat and stir well.

**3.** Carefully pour the jelly into eight serving glasses or bowls and leave to set in the fridge before making the remaining jellies.

**4.** Make the remaining jellies one at a time as described above, and layer on top of each other to create a rainbow effect.

***You can use a variety of different juices to achieve different colour combinations.**

efore using any kitchen equipment.

# Time Out!

Have you ever fancied living in the past, or are you a perfect twentyfirst century girl? Try our fun quiz to find out what time suits *you* best.

**1.** *Mum's mad cos you've accidentally spilt your glitter nail varnish on the living room carpet. Do you...*

**a)** Storm out, saying it's not fair to make such a fuss over a tiny bit of nail varnish, and you were going to clear it up anyway?
**b)** Grin and say that you think the carpet looks better with a bit of glitter on it?
**c)** Quickly change the subject by saying that you got top marks in the weekly maths test?

**2.** *How would you best describe your favourite hairstyle?*

**c)** Short and simple. You don't want to stand out in a crowd.
**b)** Anything unusual - especially if someone else does it for you.
**a)** A pony tail or just hanging loose.

**3.** *It's your turn to wash the kitchen floor - a job you really hate. How do you get out of it?*

**b)** Suggest your mum gets a cleaning lady.
**c)** Say you've heard it's bad to keep things too clean, as you'll never develop immunity to germs.
**a)** Huff and say that you're sick of doing all the chores while your brother does nothing.

**4.** *It's your first day at a new school. Do you...*

**b)** Get Mum or Dad to drive you right to the school gate?
**a)** Make sure someone walks you to the bus stop?
**c)** Wave goodbye at the door. A new school is a new adventure?

**5.** *Your older sister is allowed to go to the school disco, but your parents say you are still too young. What do you do?*

**c)** Announce that the head has asked for everyone's support because the ticket money will go to stop the school being closed.
**a)** Throw a tantrum and refuse to do your homework unless you are allowed to go.
**b)** Say you've been voted best dancer in your class, and it's essential you go to show the others what to do.

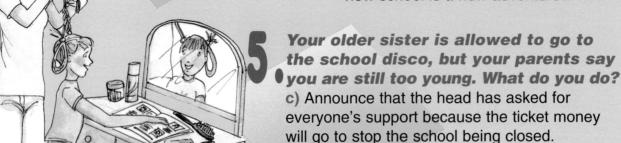

**6.** Your school report isn't very good. How do you explain it to your parents?

**a)** Say you can't be expected to get good results when you keep having to wash the kitchen floor.

**c)** Tell them that there are three other girls in the class with the same name, and maybe you've been given the wrong report.

**b)** Point to the bit in the report that says you have a strong, high-spirited personality.

**7.** You've been left out of the netball team. How do you react?

**c)** Make sure you're always available - just in case someone drops out.

**b)** Play better next time, so you **have** to be picked.

**a)** Charge out of the practice saying how bad the team is.

**8.** Your friend wants you to look after her dog while she's on holiday. Your parents say no, so how do you get them to agree?

**b)** Groom the dog beautifully, then get your parents to meet him to see if they might relent.

**a)** Dash out of the house saying you won't come back if it can't stay.

**c)** Say that someone else has taken the dog, but actually hide him in the attic.

## Now add up your scores to discover the perfect time for you!

### Mostly a
## Miss Stone-Age Stomper

You're passionate, impulsive, loyal and hot-tempered, so the Stone Age would have suited you perfectly. You like things to be plain, simple and without fuss, but you still manage to survive in your own way in this modern world.

### Mostly b
## Miss Medieval Princess

When the pressure's on, you don't worry a bit. You just giggle, flash your eyes at everyone, and hope that someone else will sort things out. Your tactics often work, though, as you're such fun to have around.

### Mostly c
## Miss Super Spy

You would have made a cool spy or secret agent during wartime. You know just what to say or do to get out of awkward situations and, although it doesn't always work, you can usually get your own way very successfully.

### A mixture of all three
## Miss 2006

The best time of all for you is now - so aren't you the lucky one? You enjoy being a modern girl of today and for you, life's very nearly perfect just the way it is. Cool!

Best Friends

# A Friend For Fay

That afternoon —

A child who spills ink over her books does not deserve a treat. You will not come to the park with Miss Regina and me!

That is nothing unusual. They always find an excuse to leave me behind.

But I don't mind. It gives me the chance to watch the little beggar boy and his dog. They come to the square every day.

His music makes me happy.

The boy looks half-starved, but I still envy him. He has his little dog, while I have nobody to love.

I have no money to give him, but I'm sure my greedy cousin will not miss one of her chocolates.

Thanks, Miss. I'll share the treat with Timmy.

At least I now know his dog's name. Maybe one day I will ask the boy what *he* is called. He's almost like a friend to me.

118

*Just then —*

Don't be scared, Missy. I won't 'arm you. This is where the 'omeless shelter, and it's no place for you.

What — what ails this poor boy?

Starved near to death, he is. Not long for this world.

Oh, no — say it's not true!

It — it's the young lady from the square, isn't it? Oh, it's a miracle.

I've been worrying about what will happen to Timmy when I die. Please, Miss, promise you'll take care of him.

Oh, I will — but you're going to get better! I'll bring food every day until you're strong.

*And so —*

Fay's a glutton, Miss Meldew. She's eaten *four* potatoes with her meal.

They're hidden in my napkin for the boy.

*And, the following afternoon —*

I've managed to save half of every meal I've had.

THE END

# Best Friends